Being Weird

Some of the greatest people I know are weird. How boring would it be without them? Not a lot in this world is for the weird, but this book is! I wear my weirdness with pride and invite you to be weird with me. Embrace the weird!!!

- Phoebe

Instagram: @realpirateweirdo
Youtube: @realpirateweirdo

*Best results with crayon or colored pencils. Some markers may bleed through.

COLORING BOOK FOR WEIRDOS

ILLUSTRATED BY PHOEBE

THIS

BOOK IS DEDICATED

TO YAYA

THANK'S FOR THE

IDEA

:)

BAG OF MARSHMALLOWS

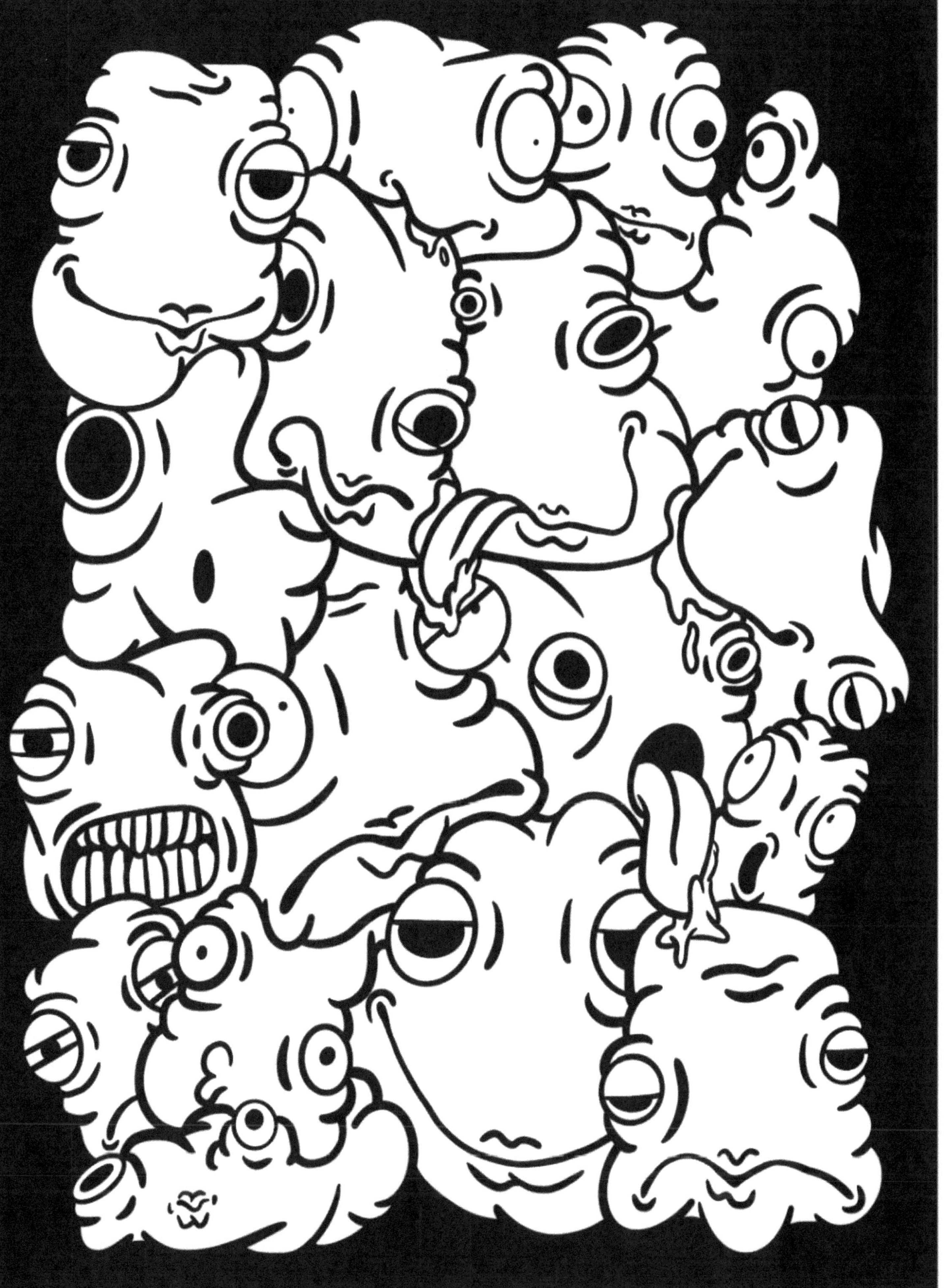

THE PIRATE

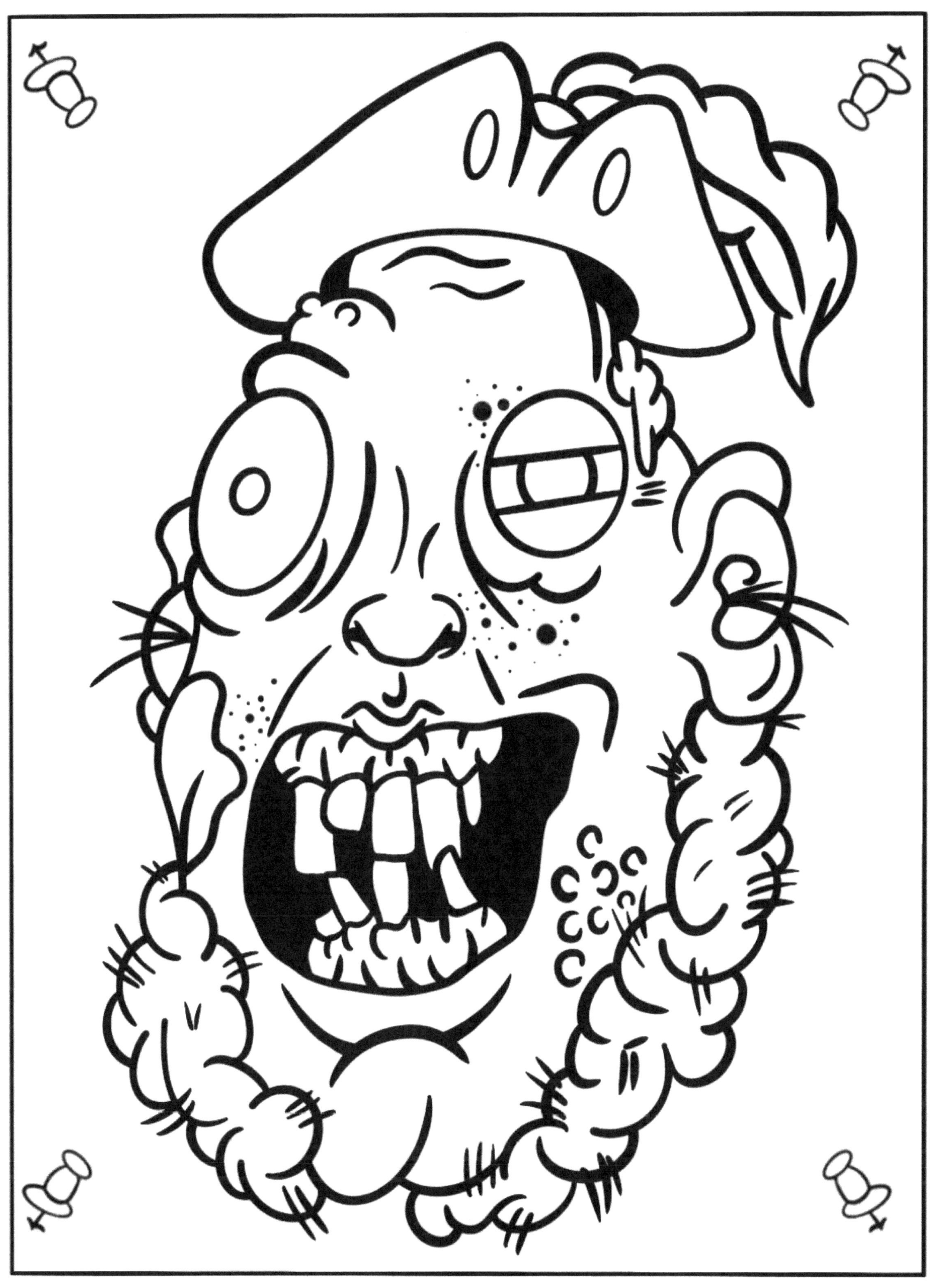

SETHINATOR

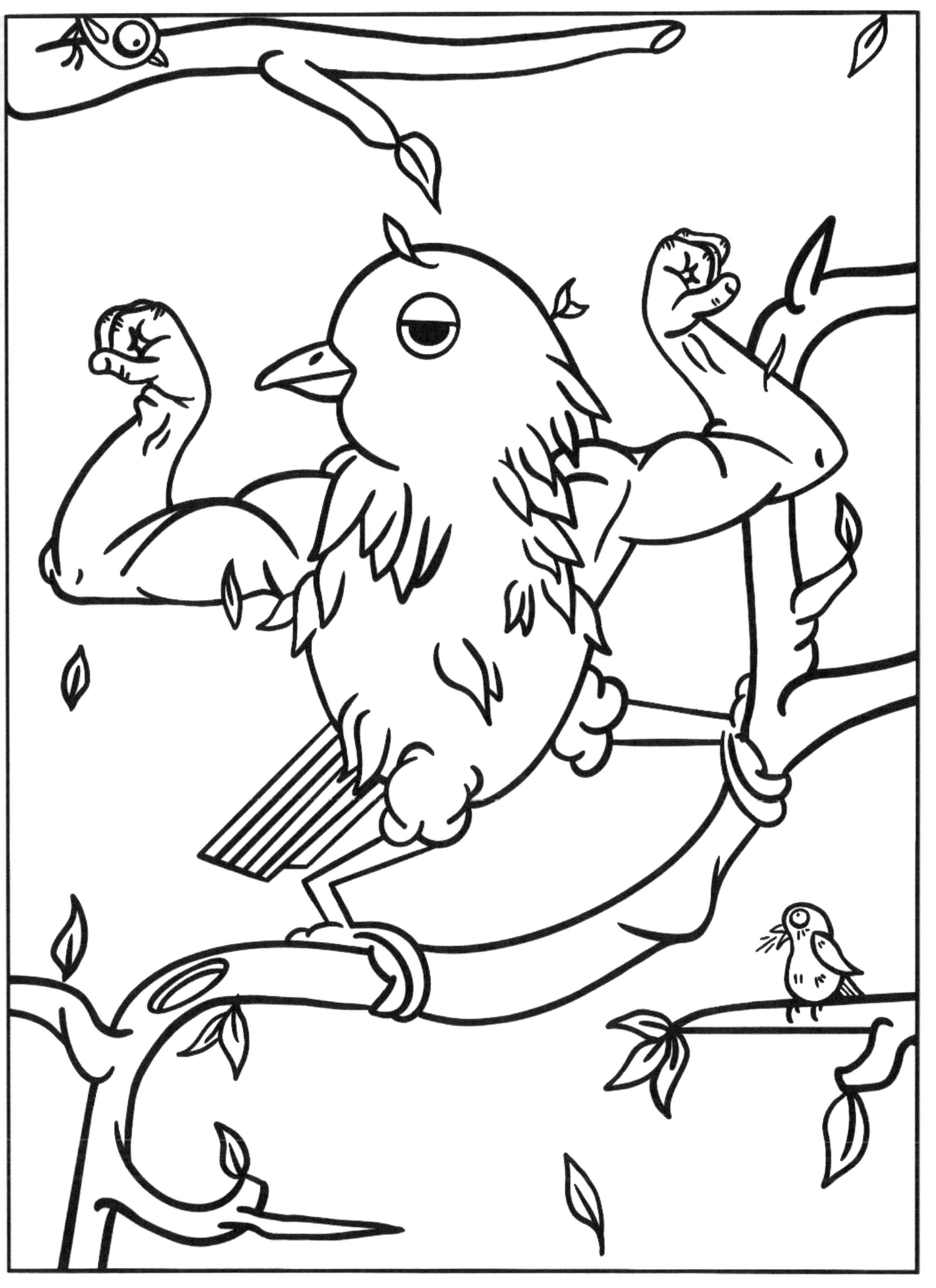

MOON LADY

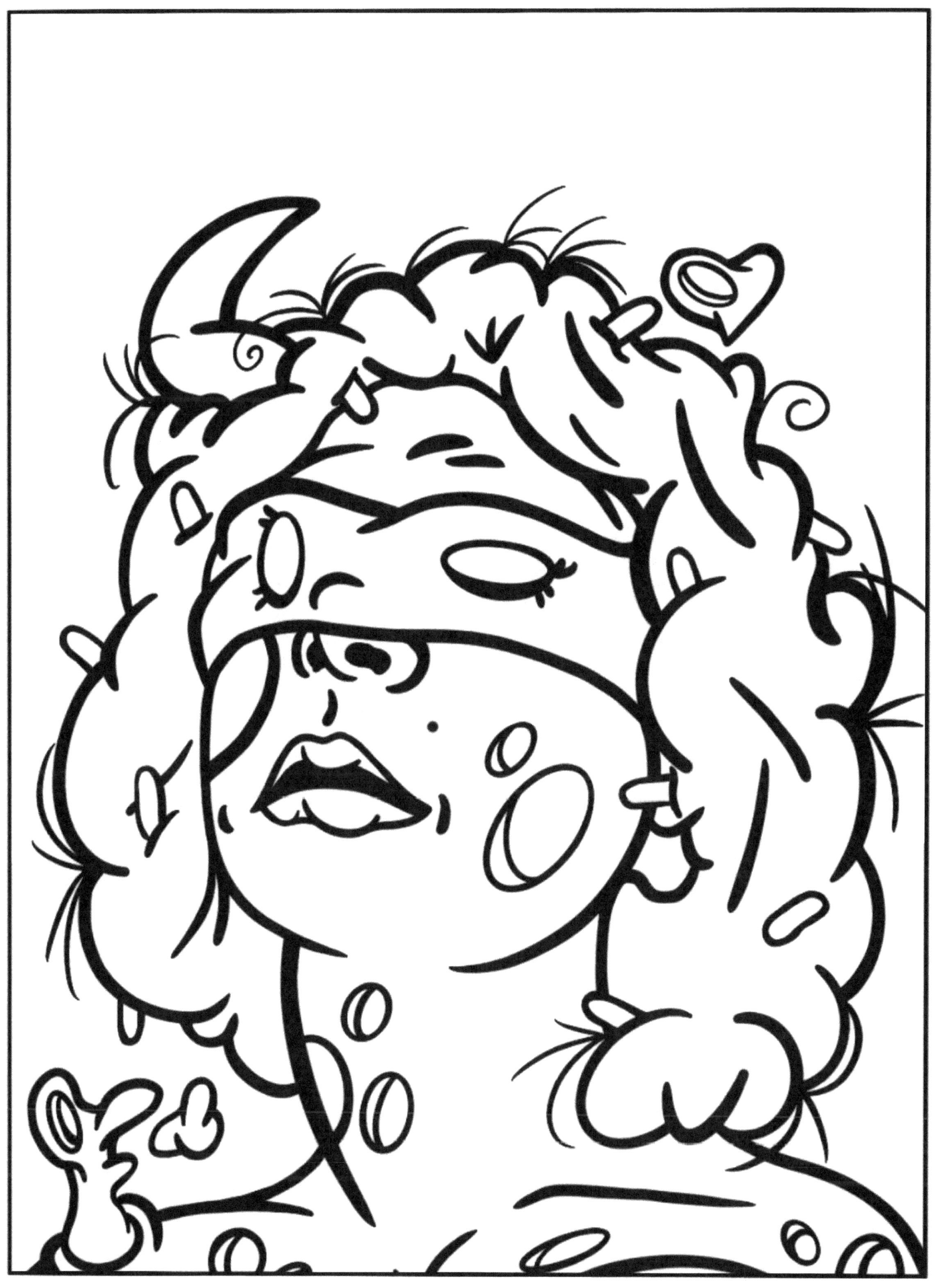

BUMMER

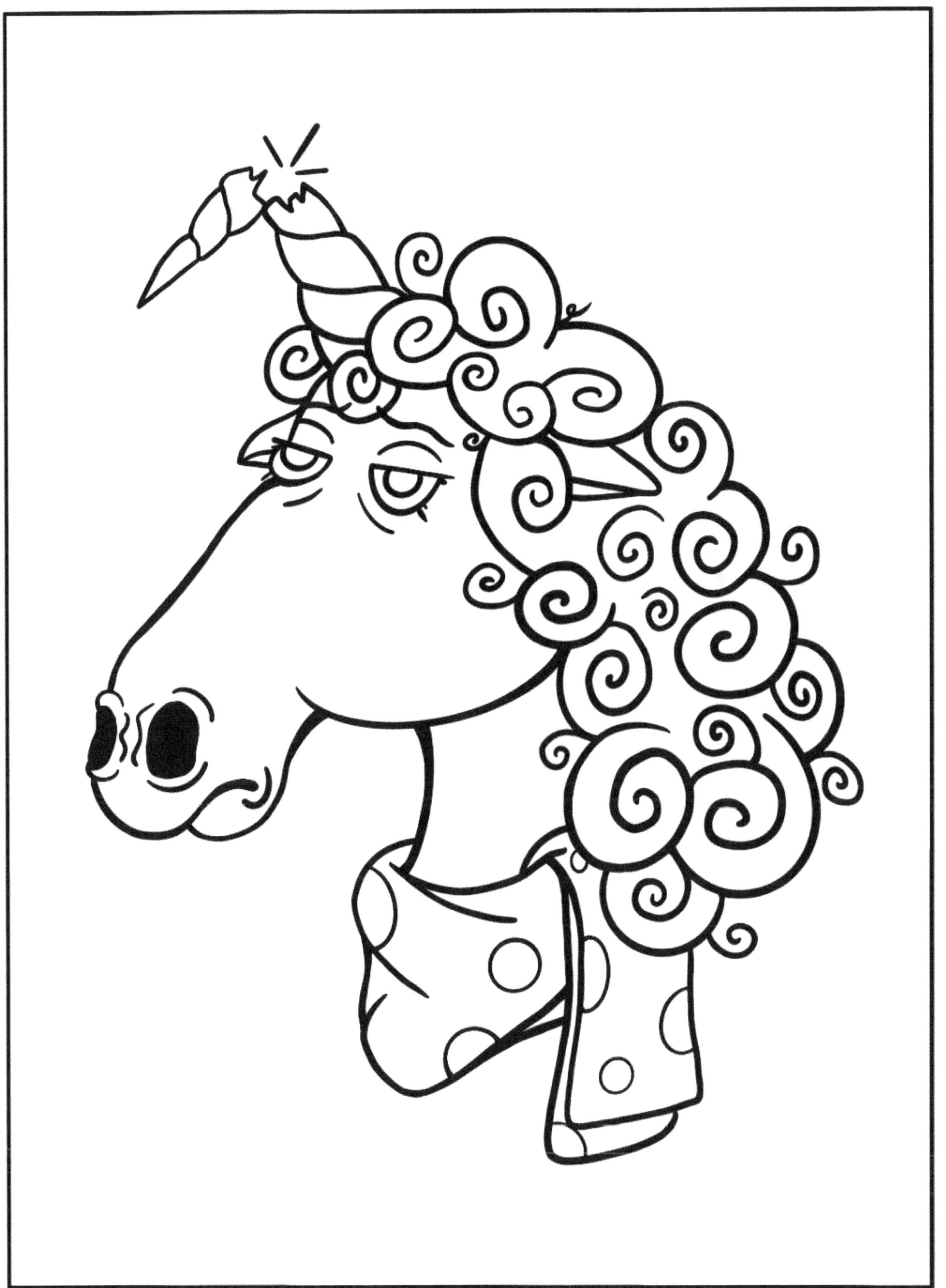

AUNTIE
Ŏ

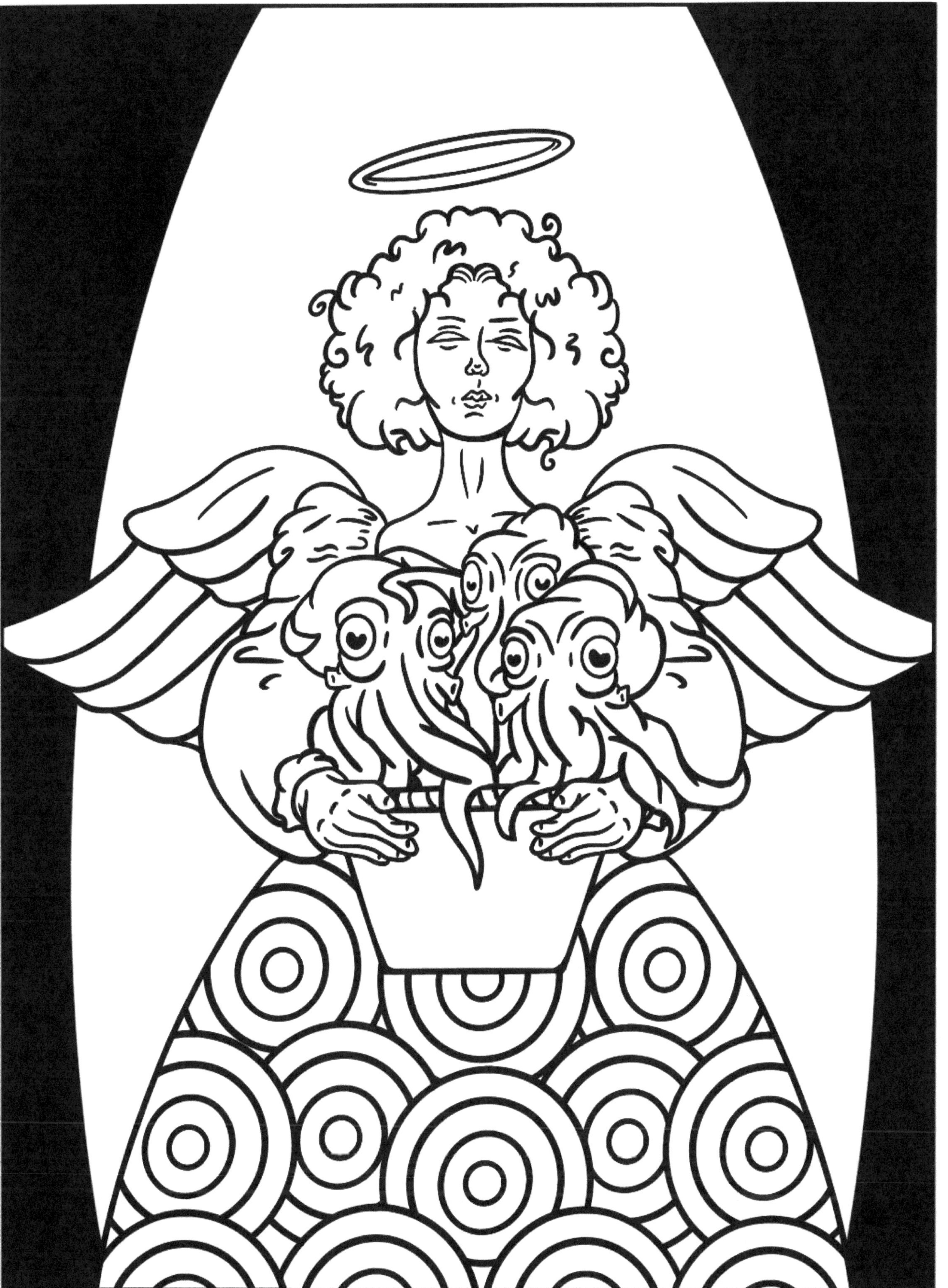

GASP...

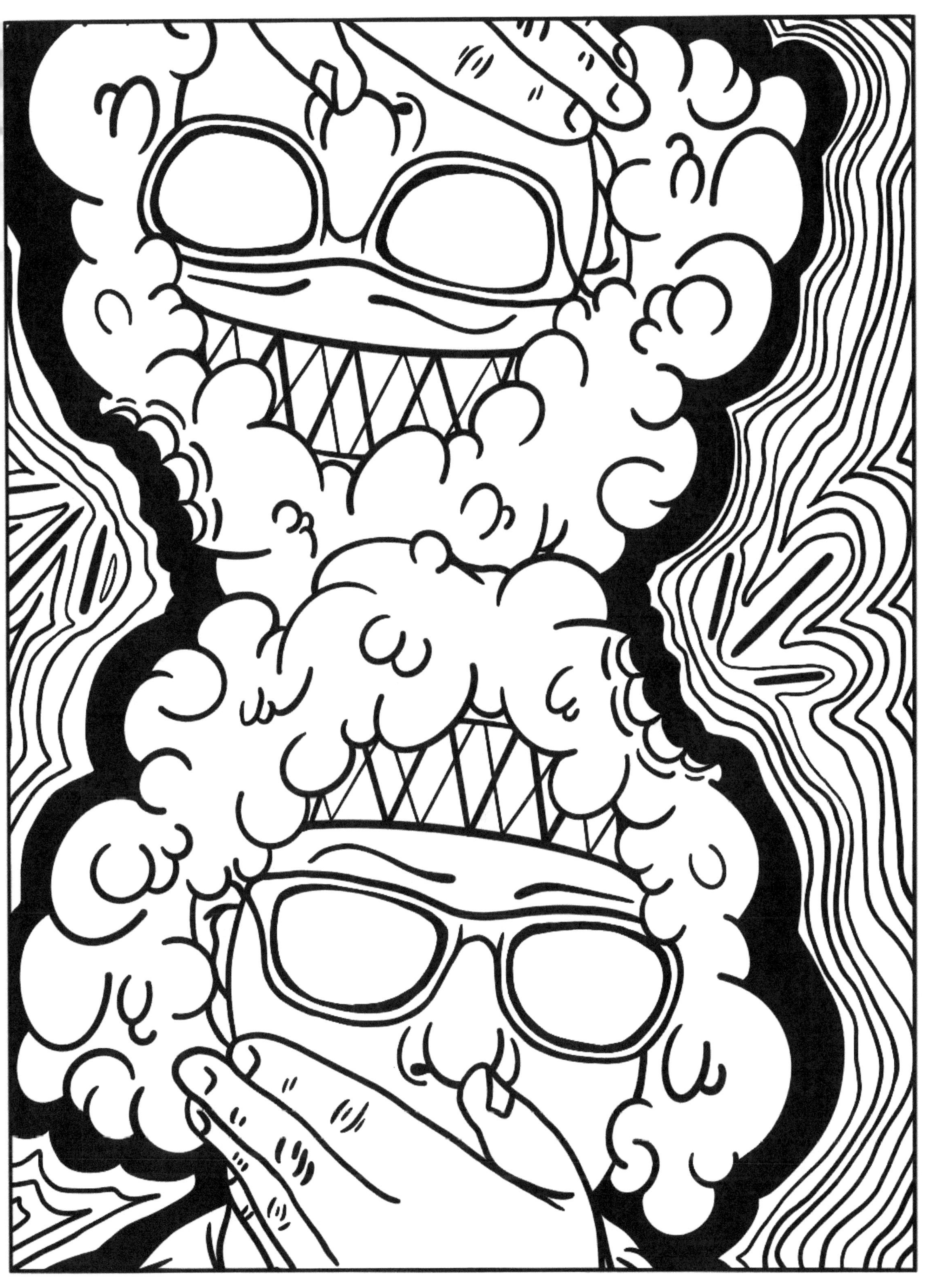

BITE BACK BARRY

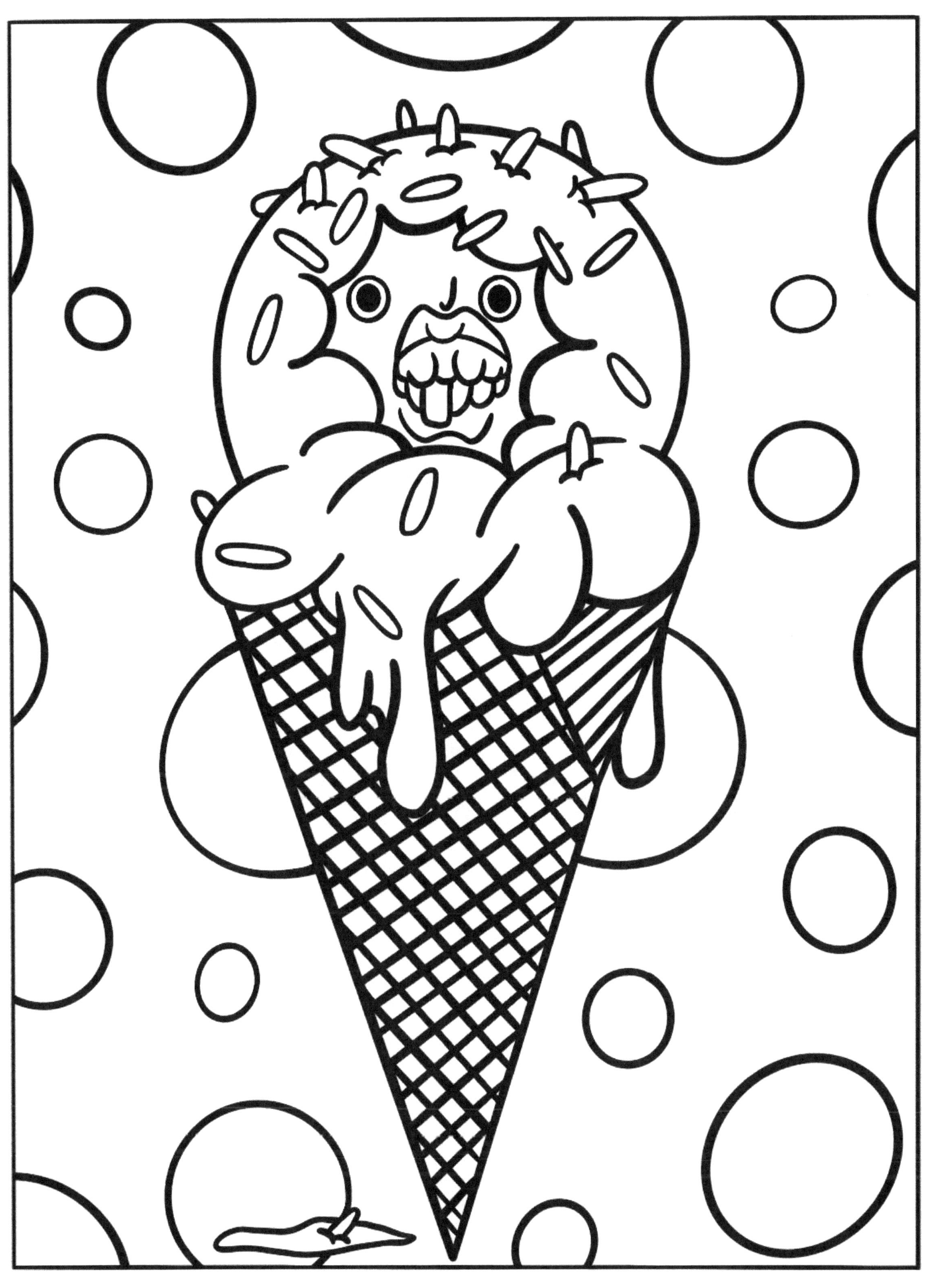

Z

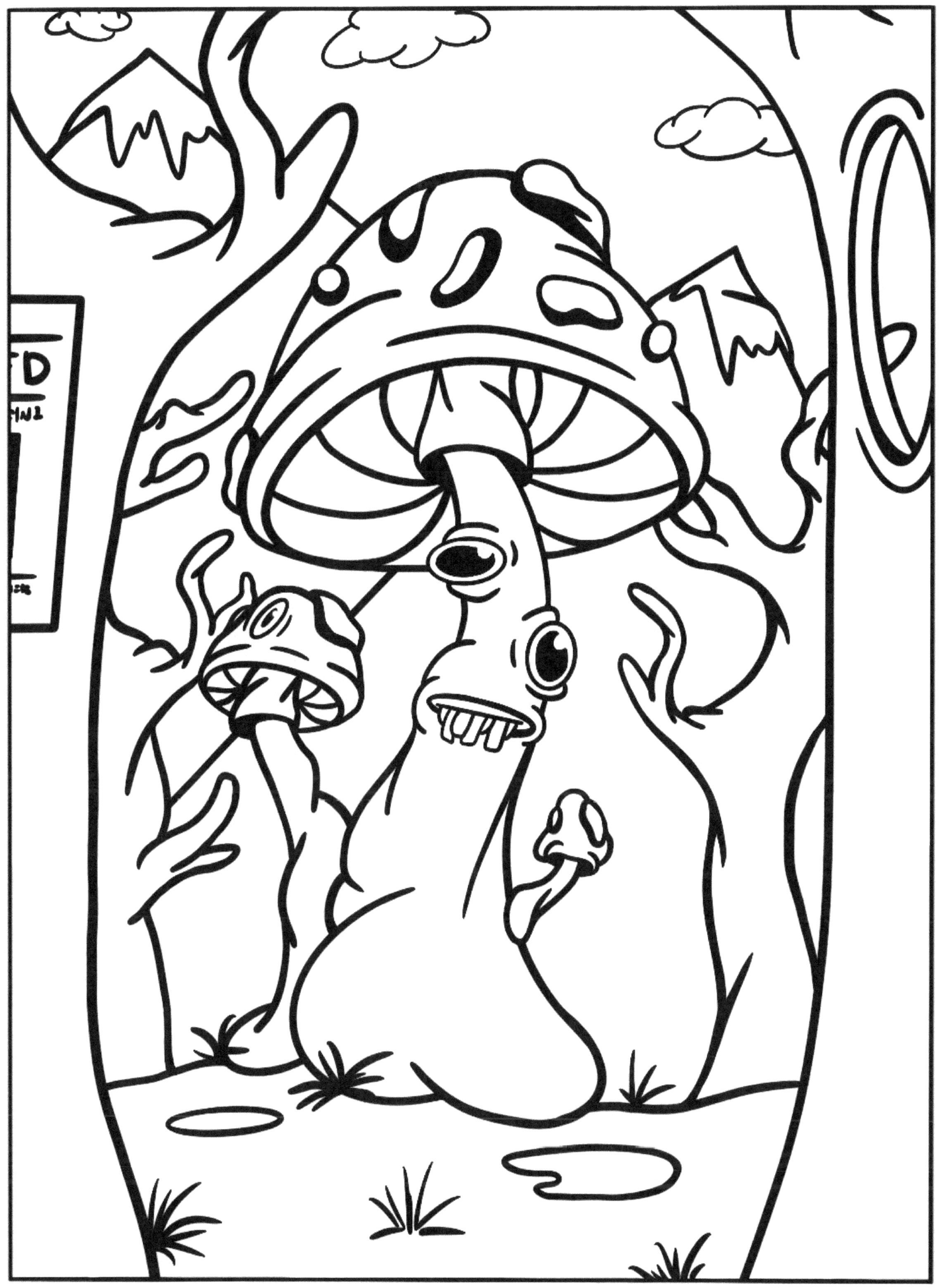

THAT LADY

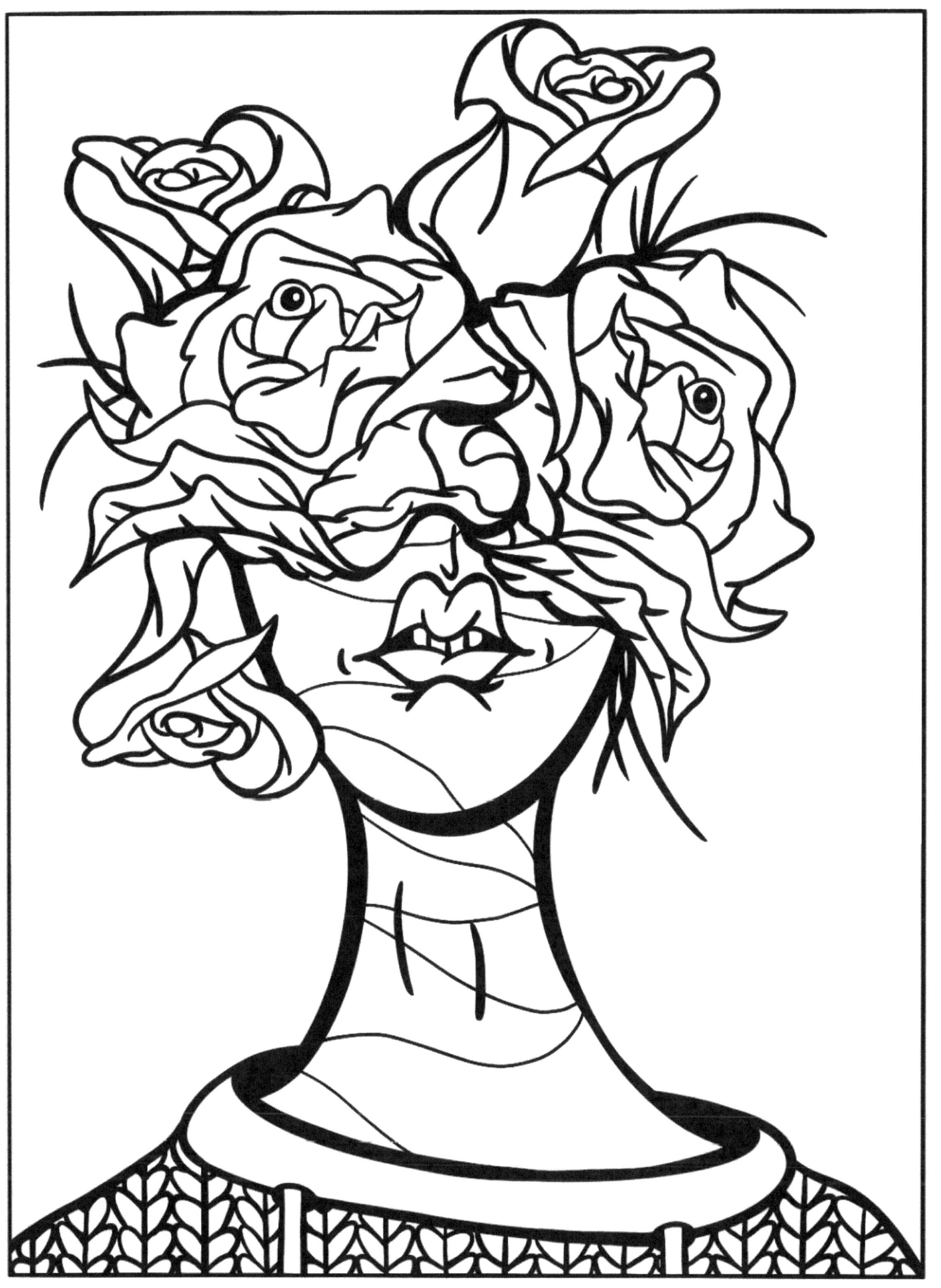

PATIENT 7

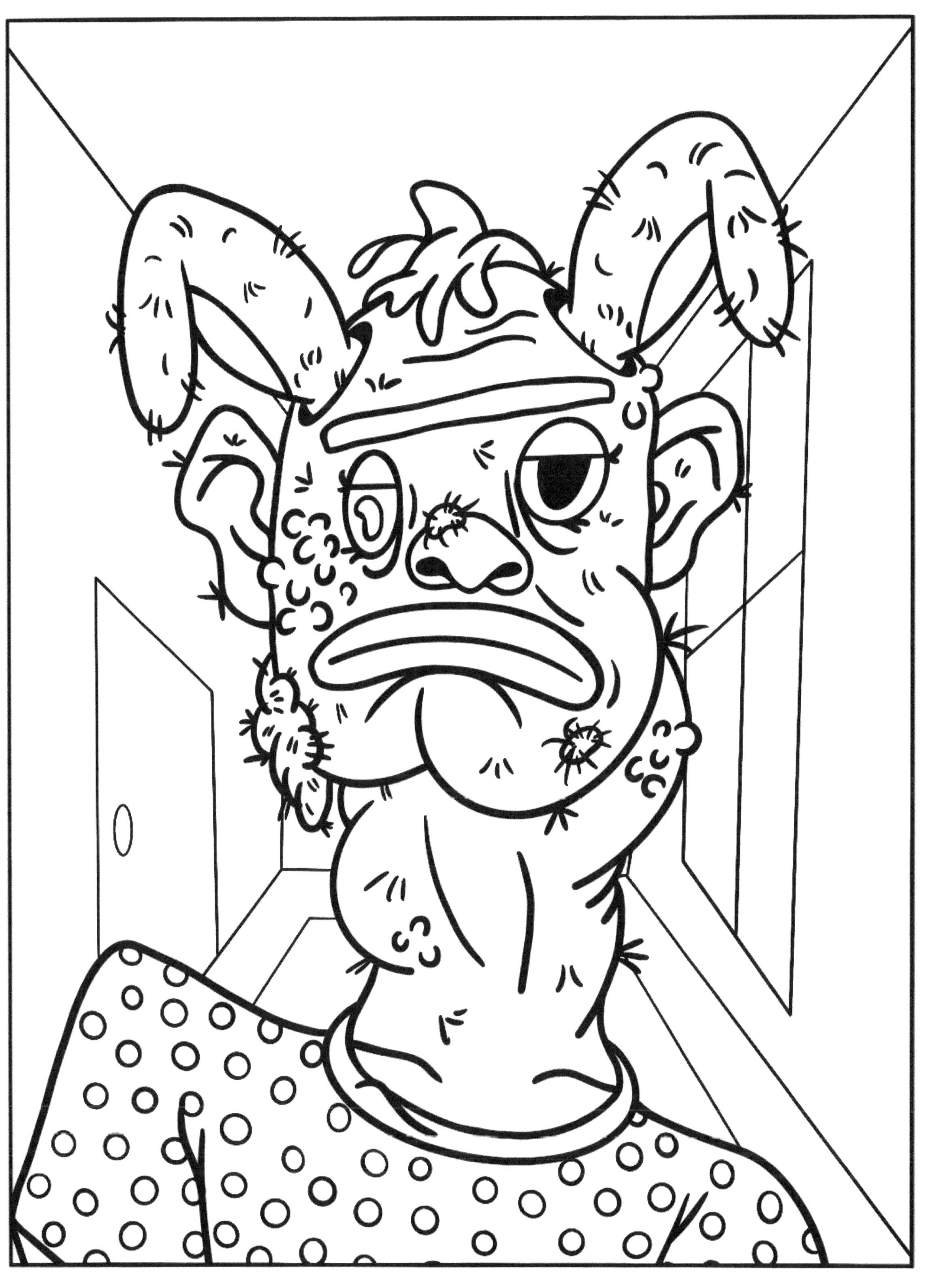

TEA TIME

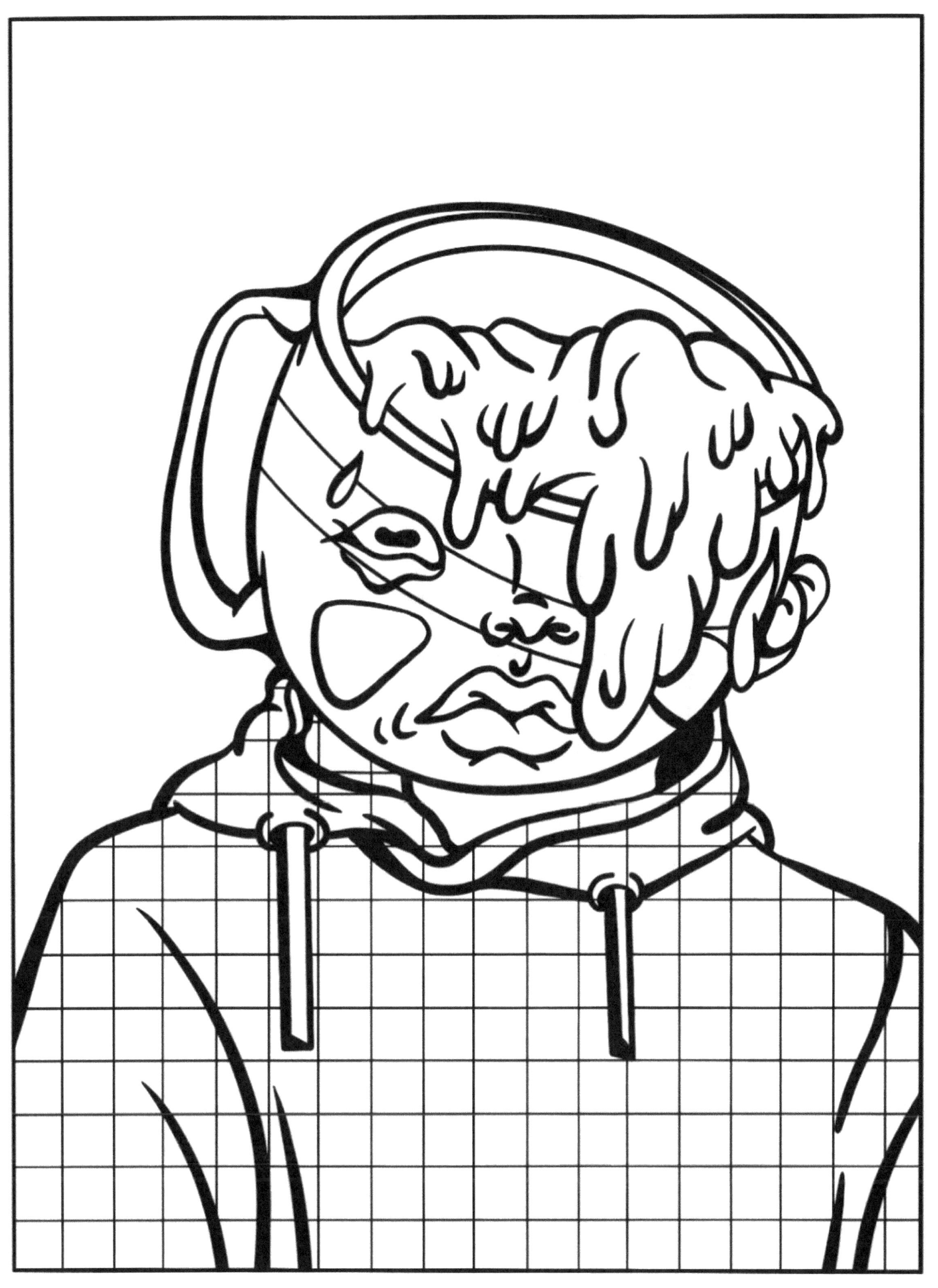

SAY CHEESE

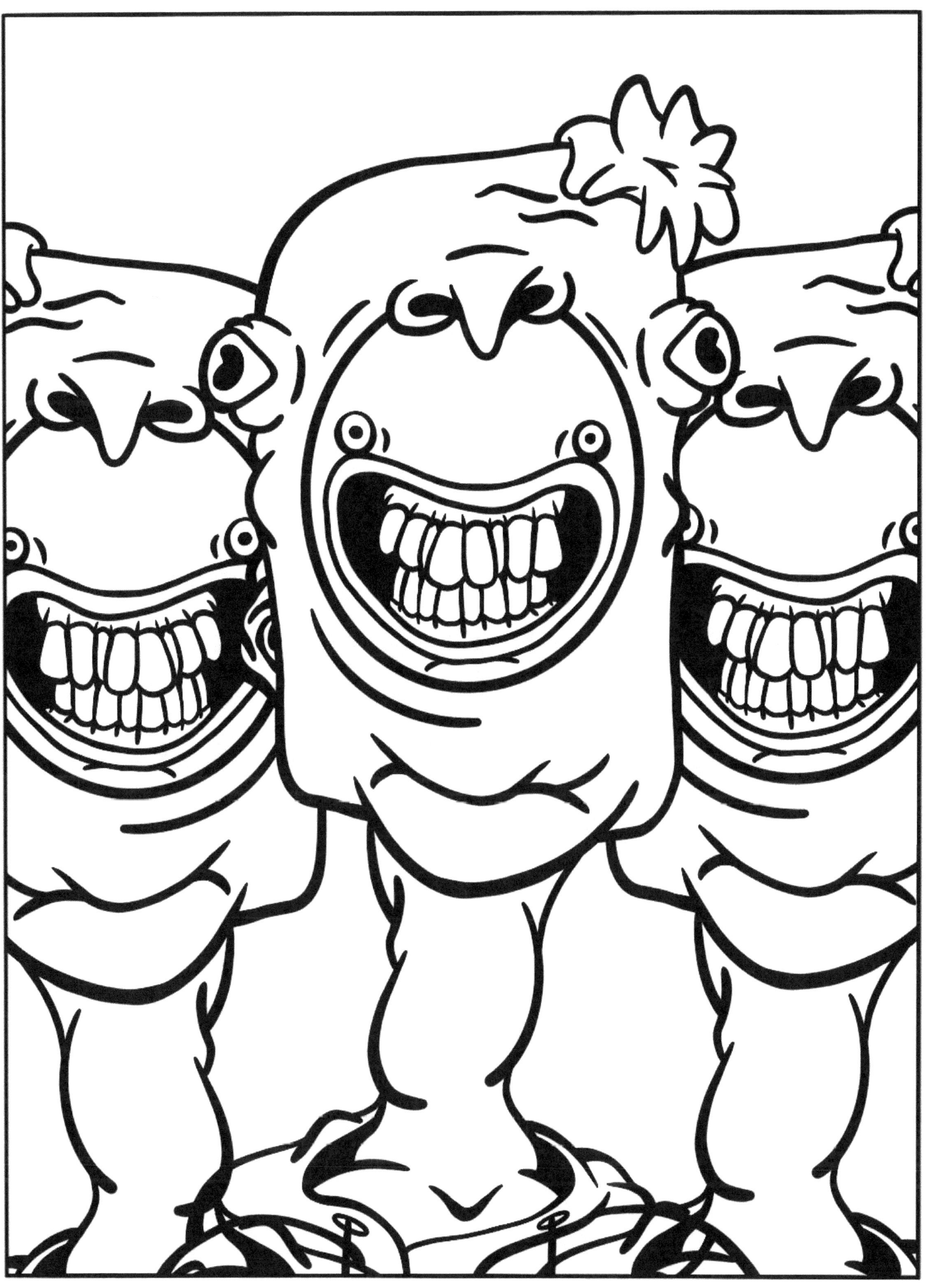

MR. CUDDLES

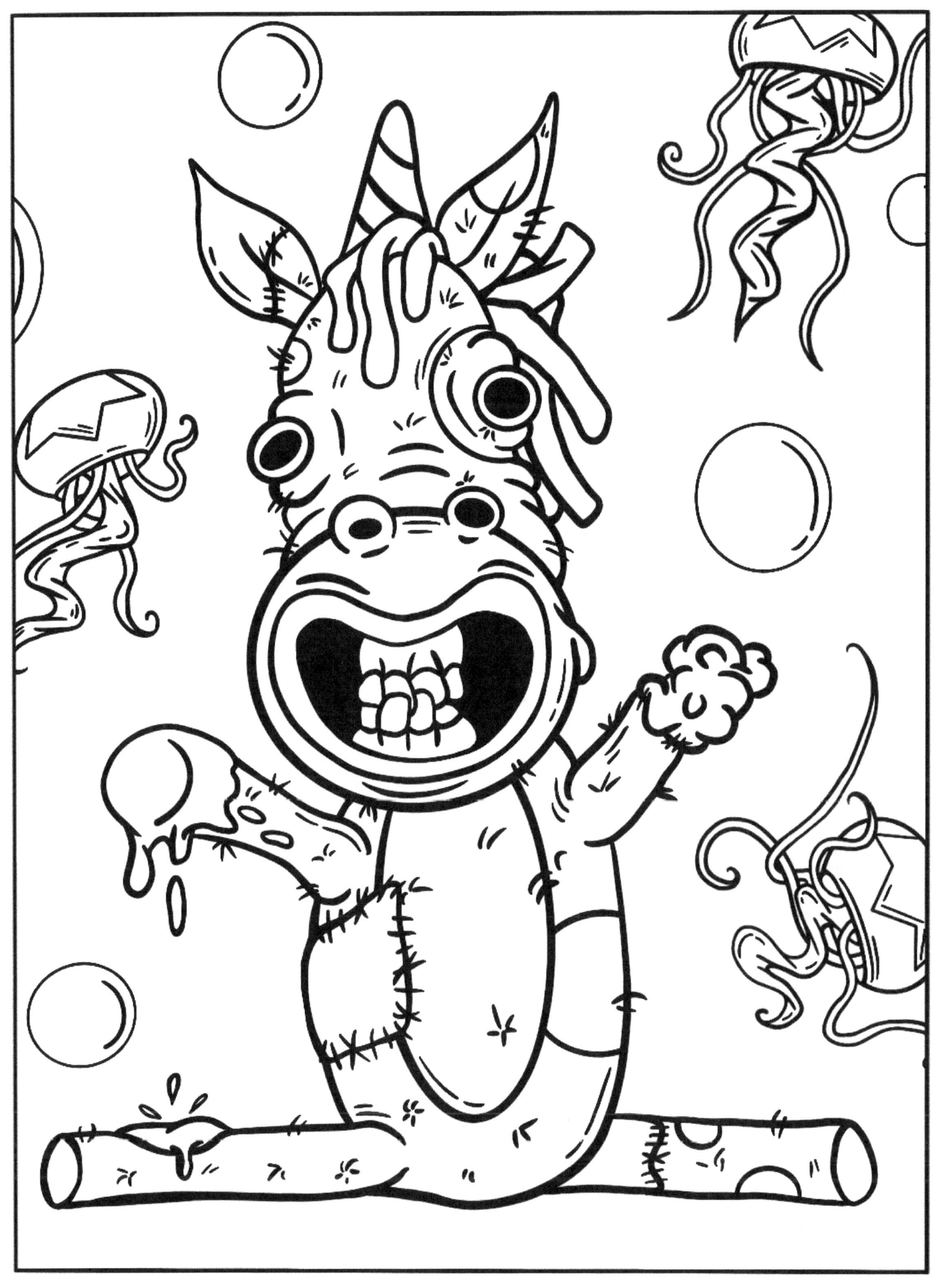

6
RAFTS

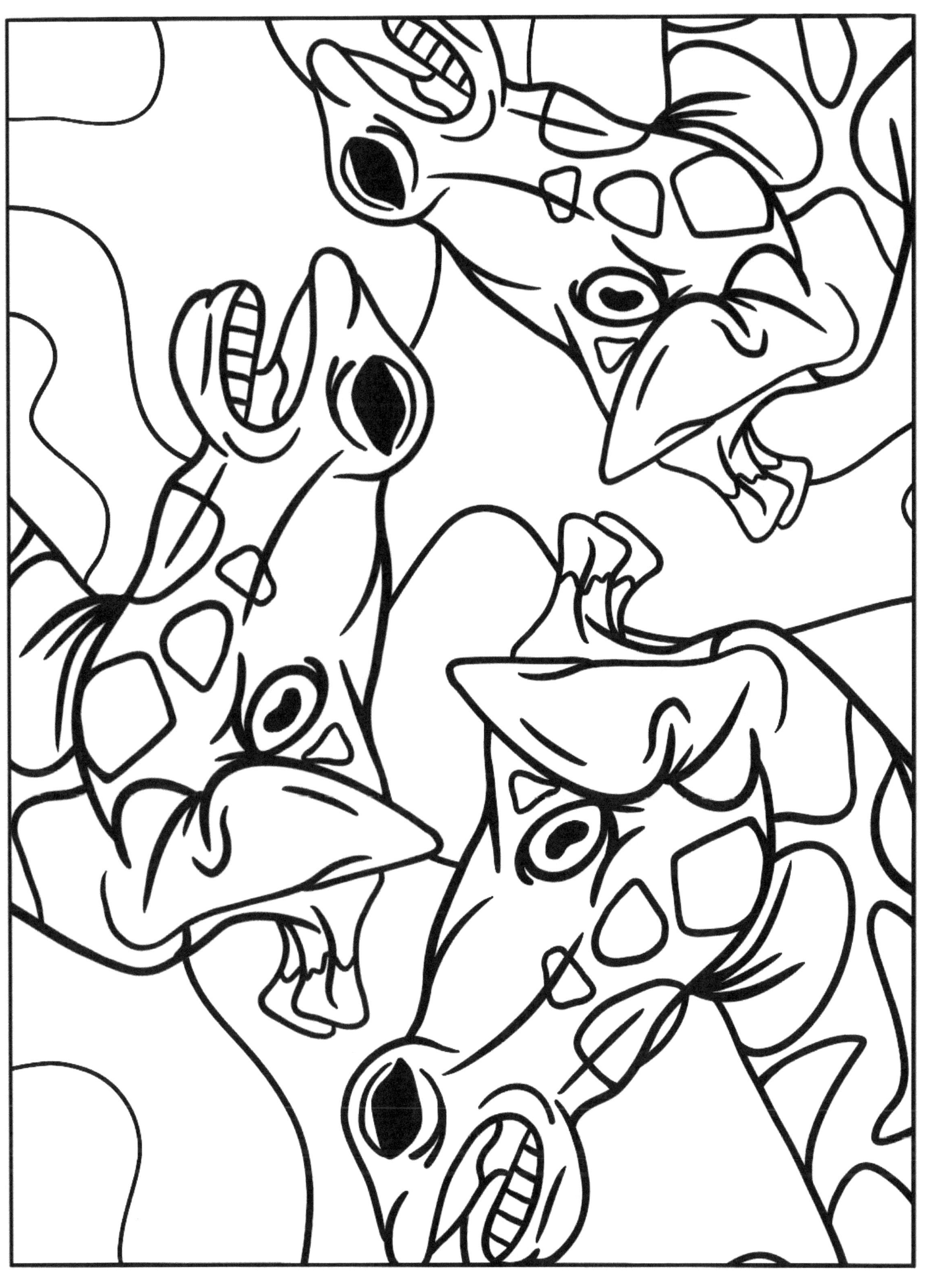

So
HUNGRY

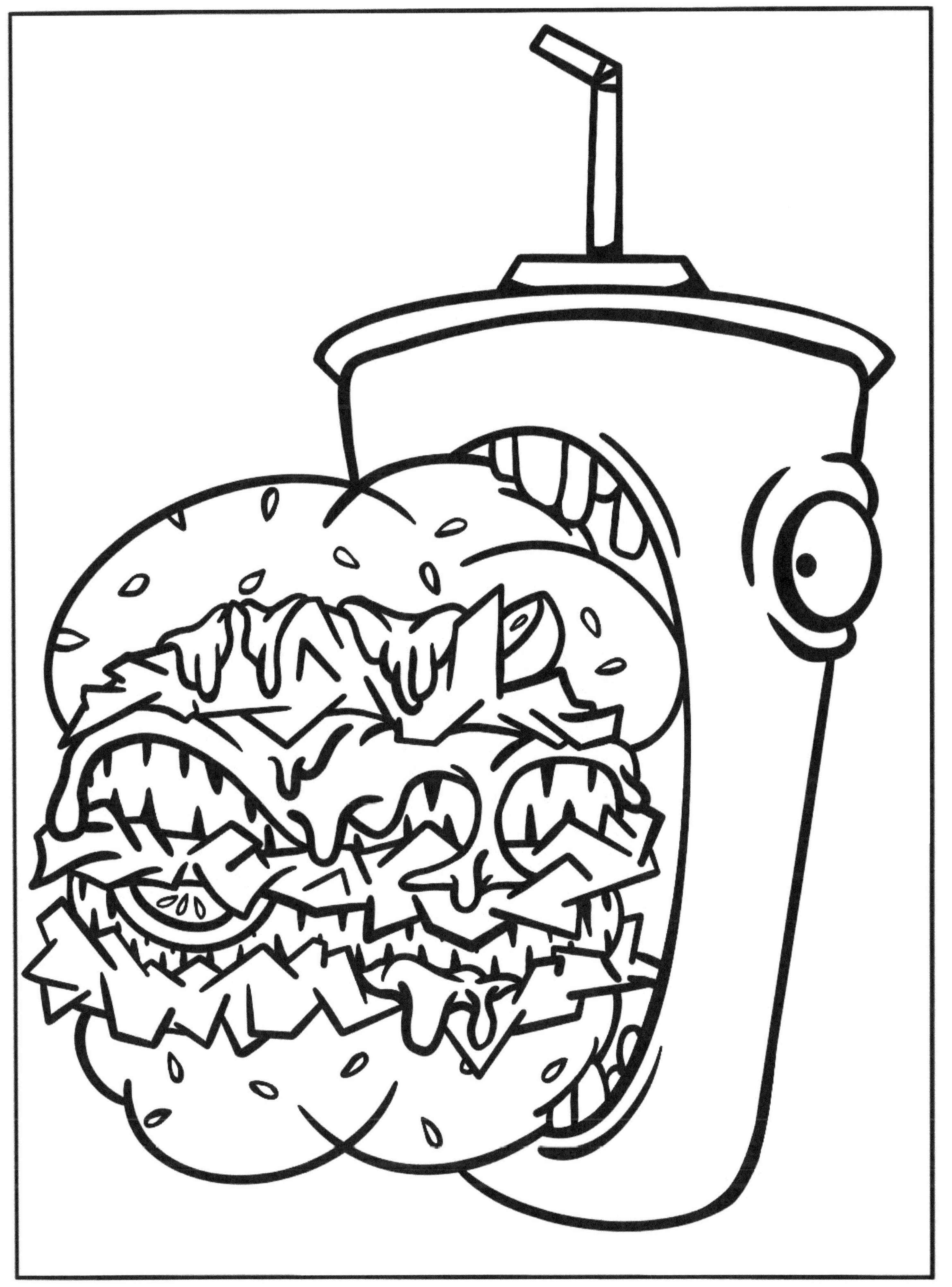

HOBO LARRY

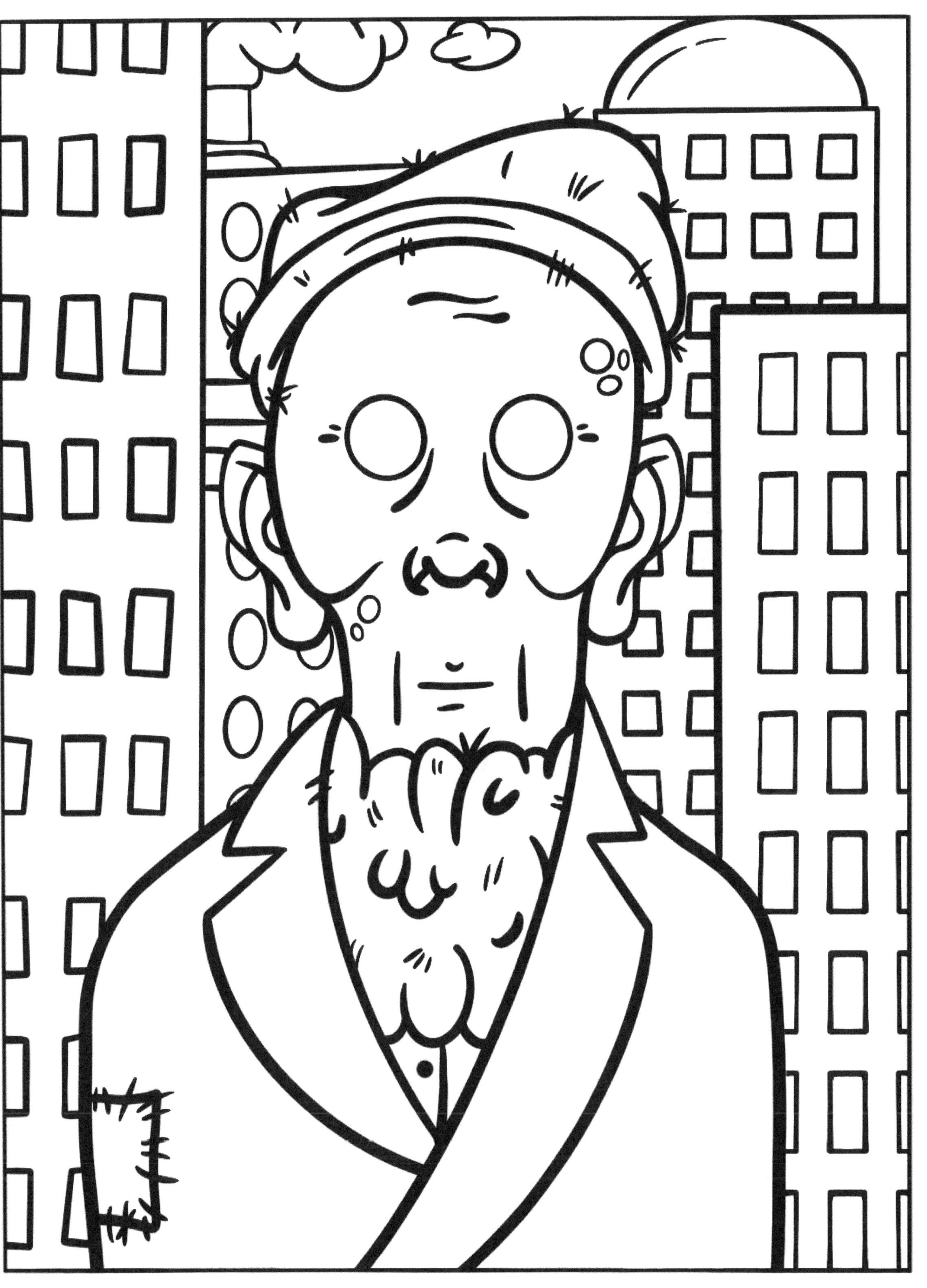

ROASTED DUCK

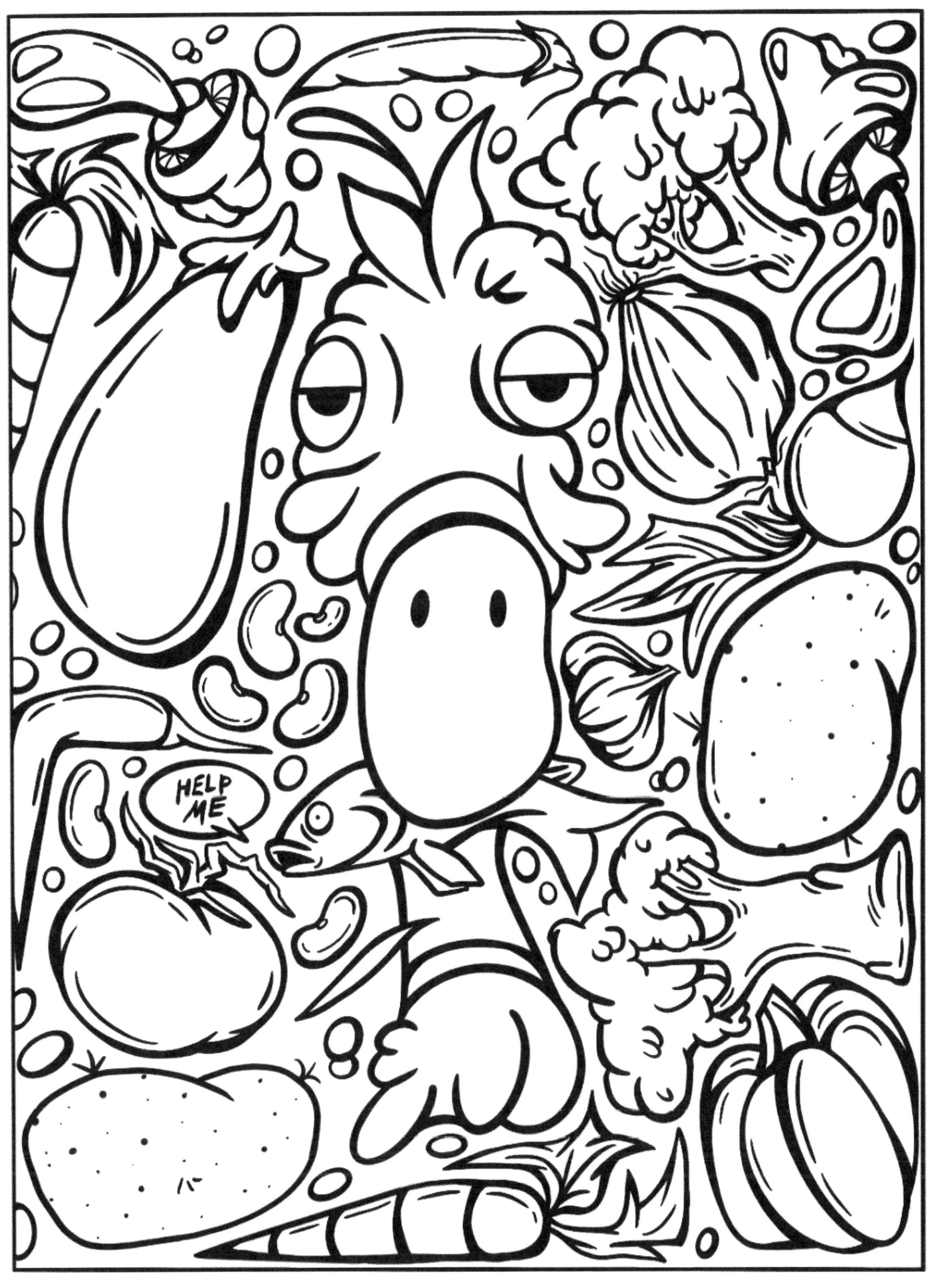
HELP
ME

JEREMY
IS
STUCK

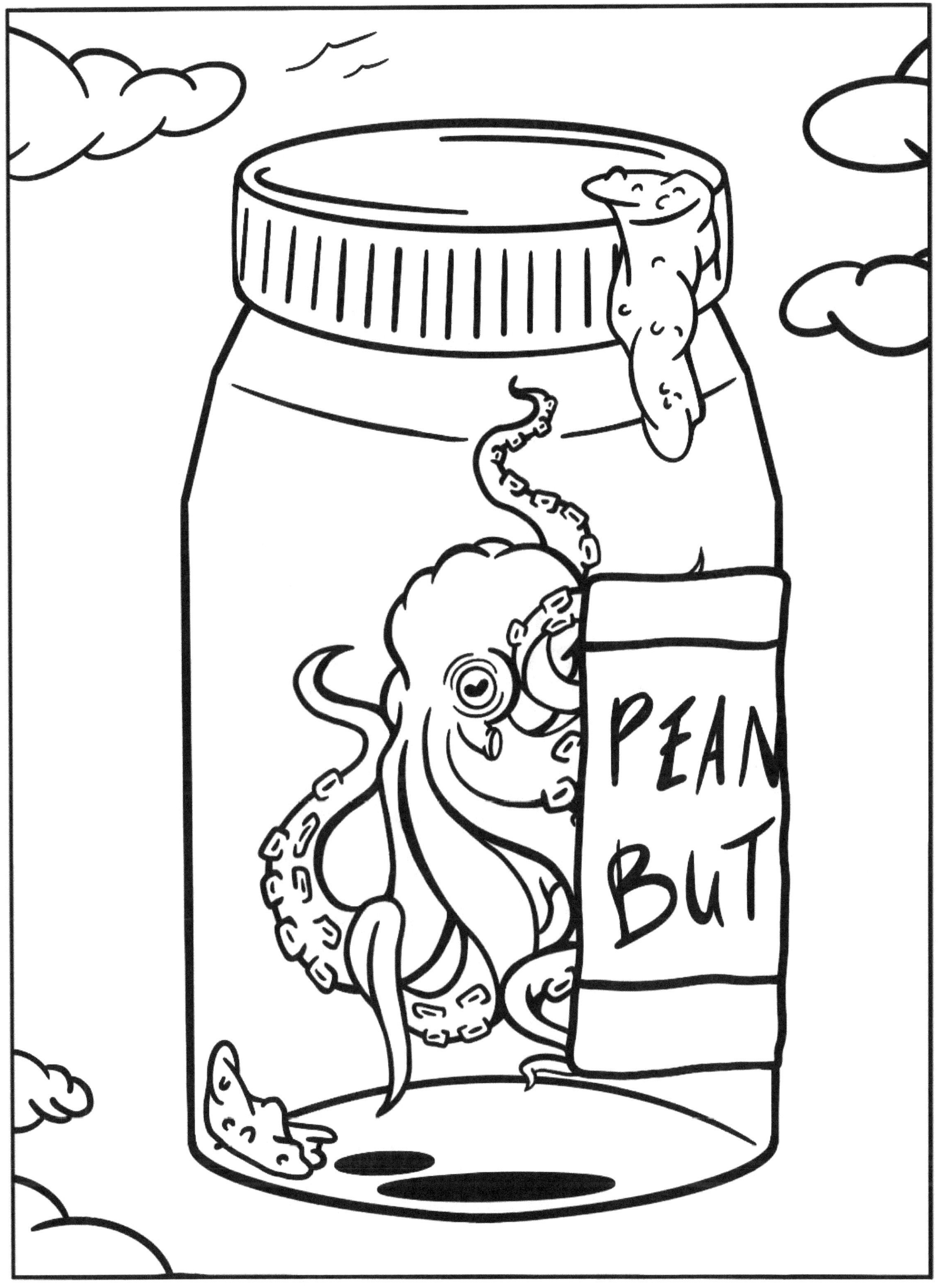
PEAN
BUT

HIGH IN THE STARS

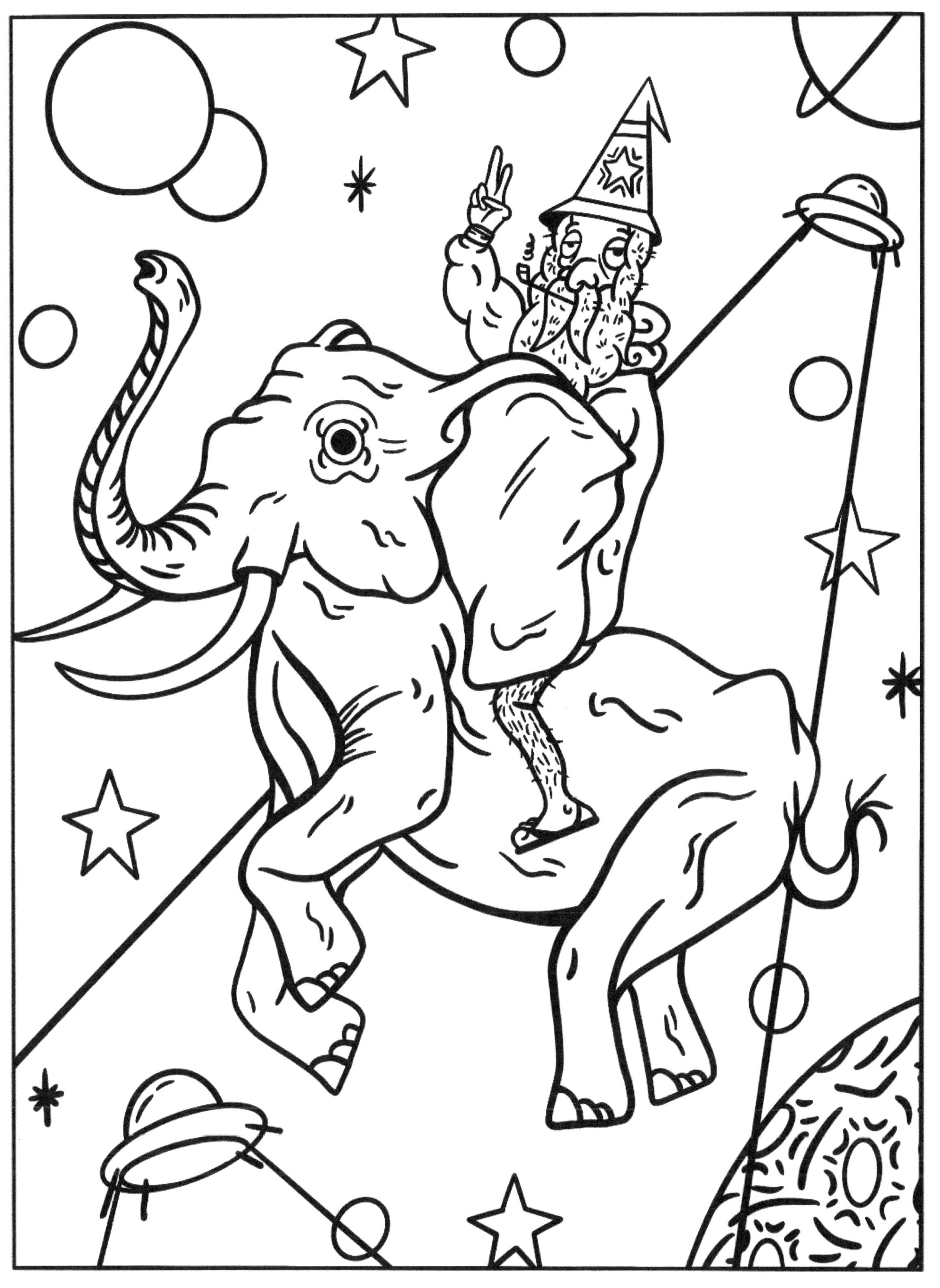

www.ingramcontent.com/pod-product-compliance
Lightning Source LLC
LaVergne TN
LVHW061258100826
845148LV00008B/1165
* 9 7 8 0 5 7 8 8 2 5 8 1 6 *